DEDICATORY ADDRESSES.

State Historical Society

—OF—

WISCONSIN.

Wednesday Evening, January 24, 1866.

PRINTED AT THE WISCONSIN CAPITOL OFFICE, MADISON, WIS.

ADDRESSES

— OF —

HON. I. A. LAPHAM, LL. D.,

AND

HON. EDWARD SALOMON,

AT THE DEDICATION OF THE ROOMS IN THE SOUTH WING OF THE CAPITOL FOR THE

STATE HISTORICAL SOCIETY

OF WISCONSIN,

Wednesday Evening, January 24, 1866.

PUBLISHED BY VOTE OF THE LEGISLATURE.

MADISON, WIS.:
W. J. PARK, STATE PRINTER, WISCONSIN CAPITOL OFFICE.
1866.

INTRODUCTORY.

The State Historical Society having labored many years under great disadvantages and inconveniences, for want of proper and commodious apartments, petitioned the legislature in January, 1865, for the use of the whole of the second story of the new south wing of the Capitol, which was readily granted, and the building commissioners directed to finish and prepare the rooms for the reception of the Society's Library, Gallery and Collections. During the year the rooms were finished under the direction of the architect, E. T. Mix, Esq., and in consultation with the Library committee of the Society. The two main rooms are each 56 feet long by 24 feet wide, and 24 feet high, which, with a hall between, 13 feet wide, are lined with shelves and cases.

At the annual meeting of the Society, held at the old rooms, Jan. 2d, 1866, Messrs. Horace Rublee, James Ross, Col. S. V. Shipman, S. U. Pinney and F. G. Tibbits, were appointed a committee of arrangements for the appropriate dedication of the new rooms. The removal of the Library commenced the next day, Jan. 3d, and was so far completed as to admit of the dedication exercises on the 24th of the month, which was designated for the occasion, and several hundred invitations sent out to the pioneers and prominent men of the state, and the friends of the Society in other parts of the country. Responses were received from Hon. J. P. Atwood, Hon. Arad Joy, Col. W. H. Watson, Gen. H. L. Dousman, Col. John Hancock and others.

While the rooms were lighted, opened, and in their best order, on the dedication evening, yet the audience was so large, that the exercises were necessarily held in the adjoining Assembly Chamber.

DEDICATORY EXERCISES.

JANUARY 24, 1866.

The spacious Assembly Hall was densely filled at an early hour of the evening. Hon. I. A. LAPHAM, LL. D., President of the Society, presided.

1. VOCAL MUSIC—*Trio from the Creation*, by some of the best musical talent of the City, led by Mr. JOSEPH HAWES.

2. DEDICATORY PRAYER—by Rev. A. S. ALLEN.

3. VOCAL MUSIC—Sacred Quartette,—"*Bow down thine Ear.*"

4. PRESIDENT LAPHAM then made the following address:

LADIES AND GENTLEMEN:—On behalf of the Wisconsin State Historical Society, I thank you for the interest, sympathy, and good will for their affairs, you manifest by your presence here on this occasion.

So far as I know, or have been able to ascertain, we are indebted to Eleazer Root, our first Superintendent of Public Instruction, under the then newly organized State government, for the first efficïent movement for the establishment of a Society for the purpose of collecting and preserving the facts and details of our history—past and passing. It was he who was most actively interested in calling the meeting that was held in the Senate Chamber of this Capitol on the evening of the 30th of January, 1864. He was, with very great propriety, called upon to preside over the deliberations of that meeting; General Wm. R. Smith, our venerable and true friend, acted as Secretary.

Mr. H. C. Hobart offered a resolution, which was immediately and unanimously adopted, declaring that it is expedient to found such an institution in our State. George Reed, John Y. Smith and I. A. Lapham, were appointed a committee to draft a constistitution, which was soon reported, and also adopted.

Thirty-three gentlemen present, manifested their earnestness in the work by becoming members; his Excellency, Nelson Dewey, then Governor of the State, consented to become the first President, and the Rev. Charles Lord, of Madison, was appointed to the office of Recording Secretary.

Gen. Smith was requested to deliver the first annual address, which duty he performed, a year afterwards, with great credit to himself and benefit to the infant society—giving an epitome of our early history, and laying down a chart for the future guidance of the Society in the prosecution of their voyage of usefulness, then just commenced.

Such was the origin of the Society, an important epoch in whose history we are assembled here this evening to celebrate.

For five long years our Society remained in the helplessness of of "mewling infancy;" only a few collections were made; only a few friends were added to our list, and few were the dollars in our treasury!

But our childhood days were numbered, when, on the 21st of February, 1854, Governor Barstow approved what the Legislature, with an enlightened liberality, worthy of the great State they represented, a law appropriating to this Society, five hundred dollars per annum, until the Legislature shall, by law otherwise direct, to be expended in "collecting, embodying, arranging and preserving in authentic form, a library of books, maps, charts, manuscripts, papers, paintings, statuary and other materials, illustrative of the history of Wisconsin; to rescue from oblivion the memory of its early pioneers, to obtain and preserve narratives of their exploits, perils and hardy adventures; to secure facts and statements relative to the history, genius, progress or decay of our Indian tribes; to exhibit faithfully the antiquities, and the past and present resources, of Wisconsin; also to aid in the publication of such of the collections of the Society, as the

Society shall, from time to time, deem of value and interest; and to aid in binding its books, pamphlets, manuscripts and papers."

Here is a formidable array of duties, truly—and all to be performed for the sum of five hundred dollars a year! How faithfully these duties have been performed, and with what economy this money—subsequently increased to $1,000 annually—has been expended, let our well filled shelves and cases answer.

From the date of this law, we leave our state of helpless infancy and enter upon the second stage of our progress, with the buoyancy and hope of youthfulness.

Rapid as has been our progress, we have not labored without disheartening difficulties; among the chief of which has been the want of suitable accommodations for the precious articles entrusted to our care. It is needless to describe to any here present the low, damp, poorly-lighted, almost subterranean apartments we have occupied, in the basement of a church. We have been compelled to grovel in those dismal rooms; and, if all desire to accomplish any useful thing; all ambition for progress; and even if all cheerfulness of spirit were not suppressed, it was certainly not the fault of the apartments in which we have been compelled to "bide our time!"

But all this is now numbered with the past—we, *to day*, open these magnificent rooms, in this splendid new State House. Our *infancy* and our *youth* are past, and we shall be "of age to-morrow!"

5. VOCAL MUSIC—"*The dearest spot on earth.*"

6. Hon. Edward Salomon, formerly Governor of the State, was then introduced by the President, who spoke as follows:

Mr. President, and Gentlemen of the State Historical Society:

The great German poet and philosopher, Gœthe, in his immortal tragedy "Faust," thus lets Faust discourse while opening the New Testament, and endeavoring to translate it from the original in order to obtain light and revelation from it for his troubled soul:

"In the beginning was the *word*," I read;
But here I pause: Who helps me to proceed?
The *Word*—so high I cannot, dare not rate it;
I must, then, otherwise translate it.
If by the spirit I am rightly taught,
It reads: "In the beginning was the *Thought.*"
But study well this first line's lesson,
Nor let thy pen to error over-hasten!
Is it the *Thought* does all from Time's first hour?
It should read: "In the beginning was the *Power.*"
Yet even while I write this down, my finger
Is checked, a voice forbids me there to linger.
The spirit helps. At once I dare to read
And write: "In the beginning was the *Deed!*"

Yes; deeds, facts, events form the sum total of the world's existence, its past and its present being. An undiscovered field, the *future,* always lies before us, shrouded in darkness, except that sometimes the philosophy of past events enables us dimly to discern the future by judging of their probable consequences. But with fleet steps the *past* constantly pursues the *future,* winning from it the ever varying *present,* and laying up its fruits and deeds as things that *were.* The *present* only has reality, the *past* alone stability. The event that has transpired, the deed that is done, are irrevocable and unchangeable, are things of the past, events of history. From them, by the inexorable laws of nature, grow the actions of the present and the future, with all their pains, their pleasures and their consequences. To profit from the past is the part of human wisdom, that by it we may mould our present and our future action. With all our existence, our civilization, institutions and enjoyments, physical, moral and intellectual, we are as much the creatures of the past as of the present, and must draw the origin of our present time and life from the past, its deeds and events.

Who is bold enough to assert that even a single accomplishmen of the present age, in art or science or any other branch of human industry or pursuit, owes its existence exclusively to the genius of this age? Every invention and every progress, however novel or extraordinary, have their foundation in something already known. Step by step only the genius of civilization advances, and however rapid his strides, his foot-prints are clearly traceable by the light of history. Men live and die, generations come and go, but their deeds live after them ; nations and empires are founded, rise and fall, but leave their works and their history to the profit and advantages of future ages.

To record the past events and deeds of mankind is the field of the historian, as wide and broad a field as human affairs are manifold and diversified. So we have histories of arts and sciences, of literature, of commerce, of jurisprudence, of religion, of wars, of discoveries, of adventures, of particular men, of States and Nations, and of almost every conceivable object of general pursuit, interest or particular prominence. That, however, which is most generally signified by "history," is a narrative of the life, events and acts of States and Nations. The true general historian is not a mere chronicler or annalist of events ; he must assume also the character of a critic, and, as it were, sit in judgment upon the actions of mankind. He must collect, classify, and truly relate the facts, must trace and study the origin, cause and effect of actions and events ; he must endeavor to penetrate into the innermost motives and recesses of the human mind, and especially of those whose acts he assumes to portray ; he must recount the triumphs, the defeats, the errors, the wise and unwise measures, the follies and crimes of mankind ; he must "set down nought in malice or favor, but present things truly." Hence it is, that the history of a great epoch, or a public man, is hardly ever justly written by a cotemporary ; because but few men are so entirely above the passions and prejudices of their own age as to correctly and justly appreciate the bearings of all things on public men and matters of general and public concern.

The history of a people, nation or state, should not only treat of its wars, its rulers, its great epochs and its great struggles, but should also draw a faithful picture of the manners of the people, their political institutions and life, their social enjoyments, their religion, their literature, arts and sciences, their laws, their virtues and their crimes, For as the life of an individual is not only made up by his single prominent deeds or acts of moment or importance, but by his character, his social and private relations, his joys and his troubles, his virtues and his failings, so the life of a nation, consisting of a collection of individuals bound together by certain political and other ties, has many an unostentatious trait which distinguishes it from other nations, and forms an essential part of its existence.

This is true of the history of all nations, ancient and modern; although when we read the historical works of some authors, we might almost be led to believe that the history of kings and princes, their quarrels, their virtues and their follies, constitute the history of the people they ruled, and that the history of mankind is only a narrative of wars and slaughters. When in other ages and other countries the destinies of a nation were depending upon the will and the acts of a single crowned head, the life of that nation was bound up in the life of that man, and his history, is its history. The history of Napoleon I is that of France during his reign, and the history of Alexander that of Macedonia and Persia while he held the scepter of that empire, for in both cases the individuality of the nations they ruled was merged in their sovereigns. But far different and much more difficult is the task of the historian who undertakes to record the events of a people with democratic institutions, whose rulers are wholly or mainly the agents of the people and are executing its sovereign will. Thus it is with the history of our own country, whose government is the government of the people, whose rulers are but its agents, whose destinies are in its own hands The theory of our system of self government has been successfully carried out ever since the foundation of this Republic, and the people thereof have been and are setting an example to other nations how a free people can preserve its independence, protect individual liberty, and become great and mighty and prosperous. The history of this free country never was bound up or merged in the fate of any *one* man. Its energies are developed by the entire people, its strides in civilization, its great advancements and accomplishments are in no instance traceable to the energy and exertions of any one man, who, by his superior statesmanship, directed the latent energy of the people. Frederick the Great raised Prussia from an inferior position in the family of independent states, to one of the great powers of Europe; Napoleon I made France, for a time, the most powerful of the European nations; Cromwell made England more mighty, respected and feared than it had been before. We, too, have had our great men, at times, directing the affairs of this nation, but the genius of our political institutions, well comprehended and sustained by them, happily forbids our having a Frederick, a Napoleon or a Cromwell. Washington and Lincoln were both great men in our history; the one has long since had the name of the Father of his Country, and the other, no less deserving, has been fitly called its Savior, and his name is called with veneration throughout the civilized world, while his mortal remains have scarcely found their last resting place. But their greatness was not the dazzling brilliance of the monarch, their achievements and the works they raised did not fall, and will not fall, to pieces with the extinction of their lives; what they did to raise and save their country remains and will remain, because it is a nation's property and not their own. The power of Prussia waned with Frederick's death; France fell when Napoleon was conquered and exiled; England's greatness was obscured when Cromwell went to his grave; Alexander's empire fell to pieces with his death; but the country which calls Washington its father, the nation of which he stands as the founder, has steadily increased in power and civilization, and even the violent death of our late martyred President, could not, for a moment, stop the nation in its onward march. The other day the bourse, at Paris, experienced a great shock; French state obligations suddenly fell; the money market of that great metropolis became seriously unsettled, and a dangerous crisis seemed at hand; panic seized the commercial world, and fortunes were lost in the twinkling of an eye, because—(be serious, my friends, for it was a very serious matter!)—because the little son of Louis Napoleon had caught a cold! Because a certain little boy in Paris was indisposed—seriously sick, if you please—that mighty empire, that great nation shook and trembled from one end to the other. Nor was this financial shock without good cause; for when the pillars of the present dynasty of France shake and threaten to fall, as they did in the sickness of that boy, French finances may well tremble; his death, the death of that tender child, might mean another revolution and a new order of things within no distant day!

Reverse the picture. A few months before this little episode in the history of France, the head of another mighty nation that under his guidance for four long years had been carrying on a most stupendous war with a large portion of its own rebellious people, a war in which millions of soldiers had been employed, in which the existence of that nation and its government was at stake, and which was just then being triumphantly and victoriously brought to a close—the head of that nation, the man who for four years had held its destinies in his strong hands and quelled that rebellion, was struck down by the assassin's hand, at the very moment when the nation under his guidance was victorious, but when public excitement was at its greatest height. There was no panic, no revolution. The nation stood aghast as the appalling news spread; but the government performed its functions with the same steadiness; quietly the successor of the deceased assumed the duties of the highest executive office. One more grave—the most honored of all—was added to the many hundred thousand in which lay buried the youth and flower of a devoted patriotic people, so recently fallen in their country's sacred cause! Uncounted tears fell for the murdered chief, but the institutions of his country, the functions of the government which he had so ably filled, remained and were pursued undisturbed by his death at this critical period.

And yet we had so often been told by statesmen and philosophers of other countries, that our system of government could not long endure, that it lacked stability, and that in a great crisis, or in times of great public commotion, it would fall to pieces for want of power and coherence. We have made false their prophecies in more than one respect; so far our Republic has proved the most stable of all forms of government. Whence arises this difference? It lies in the fact already adverted to, that in our form of government, its stability, its endurance, and the development and progress of the people under it, do not depend upon any outside impulse, or upon the energy or capacity of any one man, or of a few men who are called upon to administer the affairs of government, but it depends upon the virtue, the intelligence and capacity of the *entire people.* They hold theoretically and practically the power of government, and the development of their resources, alone in their own hands, and as long as *they* will prove true to democratic republican institutions, these will expand and remain intact. The Republic will fall when its citizens cease to be republicans, not sooner!

Thus we have illustrated why it is more difficult to write the history of a republic, the history of our nation, than that of a monarchy where the cause of events is more easily perceived. Here the historian has to study the character of the entire people with that same scrupulous adherence to truth that, in other countries, he must bestow upon the character of the reigning prince whose will or whim shapes the destiny of his people. Our public debates, in and out of the legislative halls, our widely diffused public organs, the newspapers, the individual character of our prominent public men, our ordinary pursuits, our political campaigns preceding every important election, the acts of our highest executive officers, both state and national, our constitution and system of laws, the administration of justice, our system of education, all these and many other subjects in which the character of the people and their institutions are brought to public life, must be carefully investigated and studied by the future historian who undertakes to write the history of our own time and country.

I may be permitted to advert here, for further illustration, to another subject which for the past five years has engrossed the attention of this nation, and which in future will form one of the most interesting chapters in the history of our country—the southern rebellion, its causes and its suppression by the gigantic war just closed. It is now, I believe, universally acknowledged that the cause of this fearful rebellion was the institution of African slavery, on which was built in a great measure, or supposed at least to rest, the wealth and power of the rebellious states. Many, it is true, have maintained that this rebellion and this war would have been avoided if there had not been in the northern states an ever increasing anti-slavery sentiment and agitation, while others as strongly assert that the immediate cause of the war was the growing pro-slavery sentiment of the south, and the demands and insolence of those who were wedded to an extension and perpetuation of slavery. Both assertions, I believe, are true.

Had the North yielded to the demands of the slave-holding power, slavery would have become nationalized, and the South would not have rebelled; and, on the other hand, if the extention and perpetuation of slavery had not been the end and aim of all southern political exertions; if the people of the South had yielded to the anti slavery sentiment of the northern people, and I may well say of the civilized world, no war would have desolated their fair land, hurling slavery from its throne by fire and sword, and forever burying it under the ruins of its false and wicked greatness. But it was written in the book of fate, that this fierce contest should arise to annihilate a wrong, which otherwise, under the most favorable circumstances, could not have been peacefully abrogated for generations to come, since the Constitution in times of peace forbade an interference on the part of Congress with the domestic affairs of the States. When the slave-holders found that they were defeated in their schemes of extending and nationalizing their fell institution, they made rebellion and raised war against the very Government which had sheltered, and protected, and never wronged them. To them may now fitly be applied Milton's words which he wrote of the rebellion in Heaven, waged against the Most High by Satan, who

> "When impious aim
> Against the throne and monarchy of God,
> Raised impious war in Heaven, and battle proud,
> With vain attempt. Him the Almighty Power
> Hurl'd headlong flaming from the etherial sky,
> With hideous ruin and combustion."

As our government is one of the *people*, so this war was *the people's war;* it proved *their* power and strength and resources, their devotion and endurance. It is a fact well worthy of note, that the fiercer and hotter and bloodier the contest grew, the more sacrifices it demanded, the more determined became the people in support of its government. The triumphant majority by which Mr. Lincoln was re-elected President in 1864 exceeded by far that which made him President four years before that time. I need not remind you, my friends, of the exciting scenes through which we all passed during this war, how by hundred thousands only were counted the men that the Government again and again demanded and received; how the father followed his son to avenge his death, and the brother his brother to fight side by side with him; how battle followed battle in swift and terrible succession; how the brave citizen soldiers never faltered, but shed their heart's blood, and laid down their noble lives upon the altar of their country, without murmur or complaint; how the mothers and sisters and wives of our brave soldiers vied with them in their devotion and patriotism, and succored, aided and nursed the sick and wounded; how from a peaceful nation of farmers and merchants and mechanics we had suddenly become the most warlike people of the world, in order to maintain, what was most dear to us, our country, its Government and free institutions.

One day, when I had the honor to occupy the executive chair in yonder room below in this capitol, a woman came to me, and with trembliмg voice asked for a writing from me that she might go unhindered far down to the seat of carnage and destruction, to bring home her only brother who was lingering at the point of death in a hospital on the banks of the Mississippi. She was clad in black, with poor attire, for, alas, she had already lost her father, who fell upon the battle field, and her husband, who, too, had died in the service, stricken down by disease. Her simple request was readily granted. A few weeks afterwards she again appeared before me with a face smiling through tears, and accompanied by a young man in a soldier's garment, who was still showing the effects of past disease. "Here is my brother," she said, "I took him from the hospital and brought him home ; I stole him away, for they would not let him go with me, and the poor boy would have died down there if I had left him, He is now sufficiently restored to return to his regiment, but he is reported as a deserter because I took him away without permission. Here he is now ready to return and do his duty. I hope he will not be punished as a deserter, for he never meant to desert the flag. He is well again, and I can now return him to his country."

That was a woman's devotion to her country's cause. Many, many such cases adorn the unwritten history of this war. She was a plain American woman with the spirit of a Spartan mother. Such simple incidents show the character of this war, and their preservation will aid the student in future generations to comprehend the nature of this mighty struggle and the spirit of the people who were engaged in it.

Truly remarkable is the interest with which the great mass of the people followed the vicissitudes of this contest of arms ; with what accuracy of observation they followed the movements of the contending forces, how eagerly they sought for information from the seat of military operations, and studied the details of a great battle, and the fervor of their patriotic devotion was equalled by their undoubting faith in the final triumph of our just cause. It was not a blind, fanatical zeal which prompted their untiring efforts, and upheld their courage even in the darkest days of our struggle ; but it was the consciousness which sprang from an intelligent conviction of the rectitude of the cause, and of the power of the nation's strength ; a consciousness founded upon an enlightened patriotism and a correct understanding.

A little more than two years ago I met in one of the western villages of our State a simple blacksmith at his anvil, and on entering into conversation with him on that subject, which then filled the minds and thoughts of all, I was much struck by the breadth and correctness of his information concerning the movements of the armies in the field, the past and impending battles, the strength and organization of the army, and the commanders of corps and divisions. By his logical, common-sense views, his clear perception and accurate statement of the situation at the seat of war, he might have put to shame many a learned student, and perhaps many a blundering general, and curiously I inquired how he, the simple mechanic, whose daily toil and labor apparently required his constant attention, had been enabled to obtain such knowledge and information. He replied that it was from the constant and attentive reading of newspapers containing accounts of the war with which he generally occupied his evenings. "I have two sons in the army," he added, "and the fate of our country is at stake in this war; if I was not too old a man, I too should have joined the army long since."

Yes, indeed, it was the *people's war* when the plain mechanic, and the toiling tiller of the soil, after the performance of the day's hard labor, could sit down in the evening, and, with scrupulous attention, read and study the movements of those great armies, and apply himself to solve the problems of the statesman and the warrior.

But how can the historian do justice to that part of this great drama which the soldier performed? How can he truly relate the bravery, endurance, and heroism of many hundred thousand loyal, stalwart men and youths who fought, and bled, and suffered through four long years to uphold the "Stars and Stripes?" It is now a well established fact, acknowledged even by European soldiers by profession, who had an opportunity to judge, that the American soldiery, the rank and file of the great Union army, in every material point, not only equalled the best armies ever marshalled in hostile array, but in one important particular, that of intilligence, surpassed them. And yet they were not trained to this pursuit by long years of patient practice and instruction; from far different vocations and peaceful employments did they all come, and were hurried to the battle-field without more than a few weeks', nay, days' even, sometimes, of the most necessary instructions in military movements. And yet, this may truly be said that, whenever they were repulsed or defeated in battle, it was not for lack of courage or patriotism, but from some circumstance beyond their control, or by the fault of some commander. No danger is there that the most prominent military leaders of the great Union army will not receive due credit from us as well as from posterity for all that they accomplished; their names and deeds are indelibly written as well in the hearts of a grateful people whom they led to victory, triumph, and peace, as in the records of war; but the deeds of the others less prominent, and yet, perhaps, no less deserving, and especially the heroism of the "common soldier" should have a more enduring monument than any monument of stone or metal.

"Forget not our wounded companions who stood
In the days of distress by our side;
While the moss of the valley grew red with their blood,
They stirr'd not, but conquer'd and died."

When General Grant had executed his ever memorable and daring enterprise of running the blockade of Vicksburg, which enabled him to take his army to the south side of that formidable rebel stronghold, and afterwards to surround and conquer it, all the eyes of the civilized world were turned towards *him* with admiration, and those of the loyal people of this Republic with gratitude also; but how many are there amongst a thousand, or a million even, who can give the names of those brave and daring men that volunteered to man the ships that were destined to run this fiery ordeal? And, yet their deed deserves immortal fame. Who will collect and put in form and shape for preservation the tales of the uncounted incidents of extreme valor, unsurpassed bravery, uncomplaining endurance, unflinching self sacrifice and most exalted patriotism?

This was the *people's war*, and it is the *people's duty* to see to it that the fame of its brave sons is not lost, or the memory of their deeds die with those who saw them done. It is the duty of the present age to preserve the facts and incidents of this great struggle in all its ramifications. There is not a town or hamlet in this State that has not some facts worthy of preservation in the annals of time concerning this war, and the part which its people took in it, facts that centuries hence will be eagerly sought for, and that the historian will value to exemplify and to correct his judgment. Those who labored, fought or fell in this mighty contest, did so for their country, for us and posterity, and in justice to them, see to it, fellow-citizens, that the memory of their exertions is not forgotten.

And here it is where the usefulness of this society, this State Historical Society, receives its great importance. It should be the receptacle of every important fact and event connected with the history of our State and its people; its archives should be the record from which the historian can gather the facts for his work. What I have said in this connection, of the late rebellion and war, because it is so important of itself and furnishes the best example, is equally true of everything that pertains to the past or present or future history of our young and noble State. Whoever is in possession or within reach of any facts or things of value in our history as a State, or any part thereof, let it be given to this Society, by it to be treasured up and kept from destruction and oblivion. Things of historic value scattered among the people, and only preserved as relics in families, are easily lost and come to the eye and knowledge of but few, but if dedicated to this Society, become the property of this and future generations, and their benefit will thus be saved.

The noble enterprise of the few men who have formed and expended and labored for this Society, has accomplished much, when we consider the brief period of its existence, the meagre resources at its command, and the obscurity in which it had to toil. As the work of these men is for the benefit of the entire people of the State, both State and people should assist them, and in time the Society will be made, what it deserves to be, one of the proudest institutions of the State, and one of greatest and best ornaments.

With the dedication of its new and capacious rooms in this capitol, which we celebrate on this occasion, commences, under most auspicious circumstances, a new era in the life of this Society. For the first time, I believe, it is thus brought prominently before the people, henceforth, as it deserves, to attract the attention of every one who visits the capitol, and to be constantly before the eyes, and within the reach, of the representatives of the people at their annual assembling for the purposes of legislation. And that at a time when the value of historic researches, and of the preservation of the facts of history, must be apparent to the most superficial observer of human affairs; at a time when, in the young life of this State, as of every loyal State of the Union, we have just closed a period of most painful yet proud events, when the tattered and torn and blood-stained flags of our regiments that are here deposited were the mute, yet now so eloquent witnesses of the patriotism, the heroism and sufferings of so many thousands of the brave sons of this State, and remind us that we should have a common depository of these events. Thanks to the energy of the founders of this Society, we have such a depository. May the people of the whole State recognize its value, and assist and support it in its useful, disinterested and noble efforts!

7. VOCAL MUSIC—"*Star Spangled Banner.*"

8. BENEDICTION—by Rev. Mr. ALLEN.

President LAPHAM then invited the audience to pass into the Historical Rooms, where the ample cases of Books, Art-Gallery, Cabinet and Curiosities were examined with interest.

APPENDIX.—No. 1.

ORIGIN OF THE SOCIETY.

When an organization, like that of the STATE HISTORICAL SOCIETY OF WISCONSIN, attains to permanence, prominence, and usefulness, the inquiring mind very naturally asks — to whom are we indebted for its inception, and what were its feeble beginnings, its struggles, its progress, and its final [illegible]? This Society has had for its history very similar experiences to kindred institutions—an early organization by the foresight of a hopeful few, followed by neglect, a brief sickly existence, and an early death; and subsequently resuscitated again and again. Like a little child first learning to walk—starts a few steps, loses confidence, and falls; then carefully rises, and renews the experiment, gaining strength, and hope, and trust in each successive effort—or, like the old Kentucky hunter, his trusty gun, which had caused thousands of buffalo, deer and other game to bite the dust, once accidentally failing him, he would "pick the flint, and try the old rifle again."

The reminiscences of Mr. LAPHAM, in his dedicatory address, have revived old-time recollections in the memories of several of the pioneers who participated, more or less, in the movements towards the organization of a Historical Society, prior to, and which culminated in, the formation of the present permanent and prosperous institution. It has been deemed advisable to group these reminiscences together, while yet within our reach, and place them upon record for preservation and reference.

So far as the evidence goes, RICHARD H. MAGOON, an early pioneer settler of what is now La Fayette county, and a participator in the Black Hawk war, was the first person in Wisconsin to suggest the formatioa of a Historical Society. C. C. BRITT, now of Portage, writes under date 8th March, 1866: "My recollection is, that sometime in the fall of 1845, while I was publishing the Mineral Point *Democrat*, RICHARD H. MAGOON, of La Fayette county, in the course of a conversation upon matters of interest to the then Territory, suggested the organization of an Historical Society, to collect, from the pioneers then alive, such facts in regard to the early history of Wisconsin, as they might possess, as well as to treasure up those occurring in the future. The importance of the matter was to me so self-evident, that I at once called public attention to the project, feeling, that having been mentioned, it was already "on foot," though up to that interview with Mr. MAGOON, I had no knowledge that the subject had ever been broached in Wisconsin."

Mr. BRITT's article appeared in the Mineral Point *Democrat* of Oct. 22, 1845, and was as follows:

"WISCONSIN HISTORICAL SOCIETY.—A project is on foot for the organization of an Historical Association, having for its object the collection of historical information in regard to Wisconsin. It strikes us that this is one of the most laudable, and at the same time, feasible, undertakings of the present day. Now, too, is the proper time to move in the matter, while we have such ample facilities for getting at the truth. There are hundreds of men now in Wisconsin who could furnish much valuable information relative to the early history of the Territory, and who would gladly become members of an association of the kind alluded to. A few years more, and they will have passed away, and the future people of Wisconsin will seek in vain for the information which they can now communicate. Therefore, *now* is the time to act. What say you, brethren of the press, will you help to keep this ball in motion, until the object is attained?"

This notice was transferred to the Madison *Argus* of Oct. 28, 1845, then conducted by SIMEON MILLS, JOHN Y. SMITH and BENJAMIN HOLT, and warmly endorsed by the editors. Mr. BRITT adds in his letter—"Well, this notice of mine was generally copied by the press of the Territory, eliciting favorable responses." Gen. WM. R. SMITH writes that he well remembers BRITT's article, and adds: "I and others about Mineral Point were calling the attention of the public to this desirable matter; hence the publication in the newspaper. Nothing, however, was defined—nothing proposed; the public attention was merely sought to be aroused on the subject of the formation of an Historical Society. The several meetings which took place afterwards, having this matter in view, were, in all probability, the result of public attention having thus been aroused."

As Madison was then the focus for such gatherings, and the sessions of the Territoriol Legislature the occasion when the prominent men of the Territory met; but the brief session from Jan. 5th to Feb. 3d, 1846, passed away, and nothing was done towards effecting an organization.

Meanwhile the Mineral Point *Democrat*, having ceased to exist, Mr. BRITT assisted his brother-in-law, Gen. JOHN A. BROWN, in conducting the Milwaukee *Courier*, in which, in September, 1846, he renewed his faithful appeals, in behalf of his favorite project, in this wise:

"WISCONSIN HISTORICAL SOCIETY.—A project was broached last fall by one of our editorial brethren in the Western part of the Territory, in favor of organizing a Territorial Historical Society, having for its object the collection and preservation of all such facts as may be of interest connected with the history of Wisconsin, from its earliest settlement down to the present day. We had hoped to see an organization of this kind effected at the Capitol during the last session of the Legislature, but unfortunately nothing was done to accomplish the desired object. As the paper which first spoke of this matter has ceased to exist, and the proposition not being renewed by any of our editorial brethren, we would respectfully suggest that an effort be made to effect the organization of a society by calling a meeting at the Capitol during the session of the Convention to frame a State Constitution, to re-assemble, if necessary, to complete the organization during the coming session of the Legislature.

"The reasons for selecting the time above mentioned are obvious, for then there will be a larger number of our fellow citizens at the Capitol than at any other period of the year, and, consequently, an organization can be effected with little, if any, extra expense of either time or money. What say you, brethren of the press—aye or nay?"

Beriah Brown thus responded in the Madison *Democrat* of Sept. 25, 1846: "A good suggestion, which we hope the editors of the Territory will press upon those interested in the matter. Now is the time for action upon the subject. Facts of the greatest interest in our history can now be collected and preserved with little trouble which may, in a few years, be lost, or obtained with the greatest difficulty. During the session of the Convention would probably be the best time that could be fixed upon for this object, as every portion of the Territory will be more fully represented than it would probably be at any other time, and many of the early settlers will be here to contribute much to the information sought to be preserved." Several other papers also warmly commended the suggestion.

The first Constitutional Convention assembled at Madison on the 5th of October, 1846, and was composed of many of the ablest men in the Territory. Hon. Thomas P. Burnett, of Grant, was among the number; but from illness he was unable to reach Madison until the 14th of the month. What followed, and his connection with it, may be seen from the statements of Hon. Geo. Hyer, and Hon. A. Hyatt Smith:

Madison, March 13th, 1866.

Dear Sir:—My recollection as to the first effort to establish a State Historical Society in Wisconsin, is this: Several of the papers of the then Territory had urged the formation of such a society, and it was in accordance with such suggestions that several of the members of the first Constitutional Convention met in the Library room of the old Capitol to consult together in relation to the matter. I remember seeing the written notices posted for the call, and am under the impression that I wrote and posted the notices under which the first meeting was held. My interest in the formation of a Society was such as to leave these circumstances quite fresh, though many years have intervened.

Two or three meetings for that purpose were held during the session of the Convention, and a Society organized by the election of officers. I was a member of the Convention, and distinctly remember meeting with other delegates, and urging the necessity for such a Society; but I cannot now recall the proceedings sufficiently clear to name the officers chosen. My impression, however, is that Hon. Morgan L. Martin was chosen President of the Society, though I think he was not present at the time.

I well remember the interest taken in it by Judge Burnett, who addressed the first meeting, urging the necessity of such a Society, and he was really

the moving spirit in the undertaking. He was a man of education, and saw at once the importance of such a Society in its relations to the future of Wisconsin. Gov. Doty, Thos. W. Sutherland, Hon. A. Hyatt Smith, Gen. Wm. R. Smith, Hon. D. A. J. Upham and others also took part in this organization; and, I think, Hon. A. Hyatt Smith was chairman of the first meeting. I doubt not facts and circumstances forgotten by myself will be still fresh in the memory of the survivors of those who participated in the movement, who at that time, and since have taken so deep an interest in the early history of Wisconsin.

Very truly yours,

GEORGE HYER.

L. C. DRAPER, Esq.

Hon. A. HYATT SMITH states, as the best of his recollection, that early in the session of the Convention, he, together with Judge BURNETT, Gov. DOTY, Gen. SMITH, T. W. SUTHERLAND, GEO. HYER and a few others, met one evening in Judge BURNETT'S room, at Morrison's American Hotel, when the subject of forming a Historical Society, which had been suggested in the Territorial papers, was talked over, its importance recognized, and a meeting agreed upon; which was held in the Library room of the old capitol—Judge BURNETT, and Gov. DOTY, taking special interest in the movement. This preliminary interview and first meeting, took place in October, between the 14th, when Judge BURNETT arrived, and the 25th, when he left for home on the reception of a message of the illness of his wife of typhoid fever; his former illness, the exposure of the journey day and night, caused a relapse in his own case, and both himself and wife died the same day, November 5th, ensuing. This circumstance fixes the time, pretty nearly, of the first meeting, and the formation of the WISCONSIN HISTORICAL SOCIETY; at which there were about a dozen persons in attendance. Mr. SMITH, furthermore, thinks, that he was chosen chairman of the first meeting; that a constitution was adopted, providing for life and other members; that the officers chosen were to continue in office only till January ensuing, when the annual meeting was to be held; and that the officers thus chosen for the remainder of year, were: Hon. A. HYATT SMITH, President; Hon. THOS. P. BURNETT, and Hon. JAMES D. DOTY, Vice Presidents; E. M,

WILLIAMSON, Treasurer; and THOMAS W. SUTHERLAND, Secretary. That several meetings were held during the session, and Gov. DOTY was chosen to deliver the first address before the Society at its annual meeting in January ensuing.

That at the annual meeting, soon after the commencement of the Legislative session, in January, 1847, Gov. DOTY failed to deliver the address; and that Hon. M. L. MARTIN was chosen President of the Society for the year, and Messrs. WILLIAMSON and SUTHERLAND re-elected Treasurer and Secretary; and the newly chosen President designated to deliver the address—which, however, he did not do during that organization. As a further corroboration of this early movement, Hon. D. A. J. UPHAM, a member of the first convention, writes: "There was such a Society formed at the time of the first Constiutional Convention; but I cannot certainly name the officers who were chosen. I recollect of the organization, and of meeting several times with the movers in the matter, who were Gov. DOTY, Gen. W. R. SMITH, MARSHALL M. STRONG, and, I think, HENRY S. BAIRD, and others. I do not think much was done other than making an organization."

Such are the recollections of Hon. GEO. HYER, Hon. A. HYATT SMITH, and Hon. D. A. J. UPHAM, relative to the first organization of the Society. E. M. WILLIAMSON remembers about this early organization, and of being chosen treasurer; but pleasantly adds, that "not the first red cent ever passed into the treasury." Gen. SIMEON MILLS also remembers that a society was organized prior to the present one, and that Hon. M. L. MARTIN, as well as he remembers, was made President.

The files of Madison and other papers of that day, which we have in the Society, throw no light upon this early organization, or of its subsequent meetings. This is accounted for in part, from the infrequency of their publication, and also from the carelessness of the Secretary, who long since migrated to San Francisco, and died there. There is no hope that the records, if any were ever made, of these early movements, are now extant.

Letters of Hon. H. S. BAIRD and Hon. M. L. MARTIN do not throw any light upon this early organization, except to convey the impression, that there was a meeting of the Society during the session of the second Constitutional Convention — probably in January, 1848 — at which Gen. WM. R. SMITH was chosen President for the ensuing year, and Hon. M. L. MARTIN one of the Vice-Presidents. Gen. DAVID ATWOOD has a distinct remembrance of such a meeting during that winter — his first winter at the capital. But the meeting was probably poorly attended, and the interest waning, as this is the last we hear of the old organization; and may safely set it down as having died a premature death, like many similar institutions before and after it, for want of proper care, nourishment and attention. Yet, doubtless, it had its influence in keeping the subject alive; so that after a twelvemonth interim, it was revived under more auspicious circumstances.

"There may," writes Gen. W. R. SMITH, "have been a dozen meetings on the desired object — they all proved *abortive;* the only meeting that produced a *real birth* was that which was held in the Senate Chamber, on the evening of January 30th, 1849;" and, alluding to Mr. LAPHAM'S statement, that we are indebted to Hon. ELEAZER ROOT for "the first efficient movement" for the establishment of a Historical Society, Gen. SMITH adds: "I cannot help but think it hard to be deprived of the little merit — if, indeed, any such there be — of having been mainly instrumental in the formation of the Society."

Hon. M. FRANK, of Kenosha, writes: "I recollect hearing Prof. E. ROOT advocate the formation of such a society; but who was the actual originator, I have no recollections, or means of determining." Hon. GEO. REED, who, with Col. FRANK, also participated in the organization of January, 1849, states that he remembers that Mr. ROOT was active in that movement.

Rev. ALFRED BRUNSON writes: "I do not recollect seeing Mr. ROOT at the organization of the State Historical Society in

1849; nor do I remember who, if any one, started the ball. It ssemed to me rather simultaneous with a number of persons. Gen. W. R. SMITH was a prominent man, and the first to deliver a set address upon the history of Wisconsin; but it rather seems to me that we had a conversation on the subject before he came into it. When the ball was put in motion, he, of course, gave it a heavy kick."

Hon. M. L. MARTIN writes: "It seems to me, that Gen. SMITH had more to do in getting up the present Society than any other single individual."

Hon. JOHN Y. SMITH, while under the impression, that in consequence of the notices of the newspaper press, and the effort at an organization in 1846, that the movement of 1849 was rather simultaneous in its character; yet he would think that Gen. SMITH, from his well-known historical and antiquarian tastes, was among the earliest and most active in the enterprise.

Gen. H. C. HOBART writes: "You have asked me to give my recollections as to the person whe first substantially started the idea of forming a State Historical Society in Wisconsin. I well recollect the circumstances which surrounded and moved us at the time of the first organization, in 1849. It was talked about some time before it was founded; and I give it as my deliberate opinion, that any one may well hesitate to claim that he started the idea. There never will be any doubt about the real father who laid the foundation of its prosperity, and who deserves, and will receive, that high position in the history of Wisconsin."

On the evening of January 29th, 1849, a preliminary meeting was held at the American Hotel, Hon. JOHN Y. SMITH presiding, and E. M. WILLIAMSON acting as Secretary. Hon. E. ROOT stated the object of the meeting—to take into consideration measures for the formation of a State Historical Society. A meeting for such an organization was called for the next evening, and the Secretary was directed to invite suitable persons to address that meeting.

The speakers at the meeting on the evening of the 30th, in the Senate Chamber, were Hon. C. H. LARRABEE, Hon. SAMUEL CRAWFORD, Gen. WM. R. SMITH, and Rev. ALFRED BRUNSON. Gen. SMITH's speech was evidently preparedwith most care, as it alone was published in the Madison papers, filling three-quarters of a column. The Society was organized, a constitution adopted and officers elected; and yet truth extorts the confession, that for the following four years scarcely any better success attended the Society than during the organization of 1846. But on the 18th of Jan., 1854, the Society was re-organized, a new constitution adopted, frequent meetings provided for, a live system of operations agreed upon, which, with the annual appropriation soon after secured from the Legislature, gave it a vitality it never before possessed; and from that day the STATE HISTORICAL SOCIETY OF WISCONSIN entered upon a career of prosperity and usefulness second to none in the Union. L. C. D.

APPENDIX—No. 2.

PRESENT CONDITION OF THE SOCIETY.

STATE HISTORICAL SOCIETY.

The State Historical Society, which is in process of removal into the suit of rooms prepared for the reception of its Library and collections in the south wing of the Capitol, will now, more than ever, from its increased accessibility and conveniences, prove its usefulness to the State officers, Courts, Legislature, and citizens of the State. It is, for all practical purposes, the historical, statistical and miscellaneous department of the State Library. The Society is subserving a useful object in gathering up the scattered fragments of our eventful history, and has deservedly secured a high reputation throughout our country, for the energy and success which have thus far characterized its efforts. Its Library now numbers 21,366 volumes, bound and unbound, of which over eleven hundred are bound newspaper volumes, with a creditable gallery of portraits of Wisconsin pioneers and prominent Indian Chiefs, and a fine cabinet of curiosities. It has now become a source of great pride to all the citizens of the State who are acquainted with its excellence. If the State would grant the Society the privilege of issuing a volume of collections once in three years, it would be the medium of preserving many valuable narratives of our gallant Wisconsin soldiers in the war for the preservation of the Union. I commend this matter to your respectful consideration.—*Gov. Fairchild's Message, Jan.* 11, 1866.

THE STATE HISTORICAL SOCIETY.

The formal opening of the new and permanent Library Rooms of the State Historical Society, which takes place this evening, renders some sketch of the rise and progress of the Society appropriate.

The Society was organized in this city, on the 30th of January, 1849. Little was done, however, beyond a mere organization until January, 1854. At that time the Society was re-organized. There were then fifty volumes, all of which were State laws, journals of the legislature, and public documents, except two volumes of the Transactions of the American Ethnological Society, and a volume on American bibliographical literature. A small book case, three and a half feet wide and four feet high was amply large enough to contain these five years collections.

During the first year after the organization, the book-case was removed from the Executive rooms to the office of the Secretary of State, and was under the charge of Dr. J. W. Hunt, since deceased. That year 1,000 volumes and over 1,000 pamphlets were added to it. The small book-case would no longer suffice.

The corresponding Secretary, Mr. LYMAN C. DRAPER, was obliged to open the doors of his private residence to make room for the collection. In 1855, a small room in the corner of the basement of the Baptist church was secured for the collection. Here from year to year it grew, until nearly the entire basement was occupied. The rooms, however, were dark, damp and dingy. From them the collection has recently been removed to the airy and beautiful rooms assigned to the Society in the new Capitol.

The Library now numbers 21,366 volumes, bound and unbound, of which 1,136 are bound newspaper files. Of the latter, 138 were published in the last century, several of them by Dr. FRANKLIN, and one volume in the century preceding. The Society has, moreover, sixty oil paintings, mostly portraits; over 400 atlases, maps and diagrams, some of them giving us the vague ideas entertained of the American continent nearly two hundred years ago. The Society also has an exceedingly interesting collection of mementoes and relics of the recent war, and many curious articles, both natural and artificial, sent it from various sections of the State.

Few if any similar societies in the country can show so rapid a progress. It is indeed one of the most creditable institutions of the State, and deserves to receive its fostering care.—*State Journal, Jan.* 24, 1866.

OFFICERS OF THE SOCIETY.

1866—'68.

PRESIDENT:

INCREASE A. LAPHAM, LL. D., Milwaukee.

VICE PRESIDENTS:

Gen. WM. R. SMITH, Mineral Point,	Hon. JAS. T. LEWIS, Columbus,
Hon. HENRY S. BAIRD, Green Bay,	Hon. HARL. S. ORTON, Milwaukee,
Hon. ED. SALOMON, Milwaukee,	Hon. L. J. FARWELL, Westport,
Hon. JAS. R. DOOLITTLE, Racine,	Hon. ANG. CAMERON, La Crosse,
Hon. WALT. D. McINDOE, Wausau,	Hon. WM. A. LAWRENCE, Janesville.

Recording Secretary—Col. S. V. SHIPMAN.

Corresponding Secretary—LYMAN C. DRAPER.

Treasurer—O. M. CONOVER.

Librarian—DANIEL S. DURRIE.

CURATORS:

For Three Years.	*For Two Years.*	*For One Year.*
Gov. L. FAIRCHILD,	Dr. C. B. CHAPMAN,	Hon. JAMES ROSS,
Hon. E. B. DEAN, Jr.,	Hon. D. J. POWERS,	Prof. J. D. BUTLER,
Prof. E. S. CARR,	Dr. JOS. HOBBINS,	S. G. BENEDICT,
JOHN H. CLARK,	Gen. SIMEON MILLS,	S. H. CARPENTER,
Col. E. A. CALKINS,	F. G. TIBBITS,	E. W. SKINNER,
Col. F. H. FIRMIN,	WALDO ABEEL,	Hon. GEO. HYER,
Hon. L. B. VILAS,	Gen. G. P. DELAPLAINE,	J. D. GURNEE,
Gen. D. ATWOOD,	S. U. PINNEY,	N. B. VAN SLYKE,
HORACE RUBLEE,	Hon. GEO. B. SMITH,	Hon. D. WORTHINGTON

OBJECTS OF COLLECTION.—The Society earnestly solicits of every editor and publisher of a newspaper or periodical in the State the regular transmission of such publication; Books and pamphlets on all subjects of interest or reference; Magazines; Newspaper Files; Maps; Engravings; Portraits of Wisconsin pioneers and other prominent personages; War and Indian relics, and other curiosities; Narratives of Early Settlement, Hardships, Border Wars, and of incidents connected with the part borne by Wisconsin men in the late war of the rebellion.

www.ingramcontent.com/pod-product-compliance
Lightning Source LLC
LaVergne TN
LVHW011124110826
845150LV00008B/2244